REFLECTIONS ON THE SEVEN LAST WORDS OF CHRIST

DEVOTIONS IN PREPARATION FOR EASTER

GORDON KENWORTHY REED

Tanglewood Publishing

Reflections on the Seven Last Words of Christ

By Gordon Kenworthy Reed

Copyright 2012 by Tanglewood Publishing

ISBN-13: 978-0-9852897-0-6

Tanglewood Publishing
Clinton, Mississippi
800-241-4016

Cover layout and design by Sara Renick/Indigenous Images

Book design and layout by Martha Nichols/aMuse Productions

Printed in the United States of America

1

"FATHER, FORGIVE THEM."

Luke 23:26-38

If there was ever any doubt in your mind that Jesus Christ is the Son of God and the Lamb of God who takes away the sin of the world, His final words spoken from the cross in His suffering should remove any and all such doubts. There is so much more here than we will ever fully understand this side of heaven. Altogether these last sayings of Jesus touch on every human need in our fallen condition, and offer hope, firm hope, that God's grace is truly all sufficient to meet our needs in this world, and the world to come.

When one even faintly understands the agony and pain, physically, mentally, and emotionally involved in this most cruel form of execution, and the horror of One who knew no sin being made sin for us, it is a wonder beyond all imagination that our dear Lord spoke any words at all, and even more that

He consciously directed His final words in such a way as to be one grand benediction upon His body and bride, the Church.

I find it singularly appropriate that Luke should be the writer who recorded for us the first two of these seven last words. In His Gospel story, Luke was the one who went into such minute detail when writing about the conception and birth of Jesus. He told us things about the incarnation that none of the other Gospel writers mentioned in their narrative. He was so very careful to give a beautiful picture of the encounter between Mary and the Angel Gabriel, and to record her beautiful song of praise, which we know as the Magnificat. In his birth accounts of Jesus, Luke gives many details omitted by the other Gospel writers. The same is true of his detailed account of the trials, the sufferings, the execution, and some of the spoken words of Jesus from the cross. Do you see why it is so important that we have all four accounts given to us? Each Gospel writer shows something of these things the others omit. So we need all four to have a full account of our Lord's sufferings and death. Only Luke reports these words of Jesus, Father forgive them for they do not know what they do, even as the nails were driven into His hands and feet or as the cross was lifted up and dropped into the waiting posthole.

We seek now to comprehend these words by asking a few simple questions.

1. For whom was Jesus praying?

2. What was He asking of the Father?

3. How was this request answered, then and now?

4. What may we learn from these words and how they meet two of our deepest needs?

For whom was Jesus praying?

I believe He was praying for all those who participated in His trials and death. That would include the officers who arrested Him. Do you remember that when Jesus was being arrested, Peter waded into the mob, cutting of the ear of one officer? What did Jesus say and do then? He commanded Peter to sheathe his sword, but even more He actually healed the ear of Malchus, the officer, so we would know those arresting Him were included in His prayer. But did the Sanhedrin members not know what they were doing? To a point, but not the full extent of the baseness and depravity of their judgment.

Pilate came as near as anyone to recognizing the injustice of what was being done, for three times he declared Jesus innocent of any crime at all, but caved in to the demands of the leaders who demanded His death. Were the crowds who chanted and cried out for His death unaware of what they were doing? Were the soldiers who first mocked, abused and tortured Him and then actually carried out the execution not aware of what they were doing? Again we must say, only partially; and in the end, the leader of the squad when he saw of the darkness and all that happened and heard the words of Jesus, said of Him, *Truly this man was the Son of God.*

Every one of these people knew they were doing a terrible wrong. They had perverted justice, despised mercy and proudly killed the Son of God. Yet Jesus prayed: *Father, forgive them for they do not know what they do.* None of these people understood fully what they had done; they had actually killed the Son of God and true Messiah of Israel. I believe Jesus had them all in mind when He spoke these words to the Father. Is there more? Yes, but wait a bit to expand this request beyond the immediate context.

What was Jesus asking of the Father?

There are those who attempt to mitigate or even erase these words because of their own pre-conceived notions about the limitations of forgiveness. Some point to the fact that since some manuscripts omit these words, we are free to ignore them. Ah, but many manuscripts do include them, and there is the wider evidence that these words are in keeping with all Jesus taught about forgiveness. Another interpretation is brought forth by some who say that Jesus was really asking the Father to withhold His wrath from all those guilty of His death and to postpone their final, full punishment until the Day of Judgment.

But I believe these words must be taken at face value, without trying to mitigate their force by our own preconceptions. I believe when He said: *Father, forgive them,* He meant just that.

"Blot out their transgressions completely. In Thy sovereign grace cause them to truly repent, so that they can and will be pardoned fully." That is how Dr William Hendriksen interprets these words of Jesus, and I fully agree with him. Let me tell you why. First of all, the grammatical construction of these words is almost identical to words in the prayer Jesus taught His disciples to pray as recorded in Luke 11:4: *And forgive us our sins, for we also forgive everyone who is indebted to us.* In Matthew 6:15, we read: *For if you do not forgive men their trespasses, neither will your Father in heaven forgive you.* In another place, He insisted that we must love our enemies, saying:

Love your enemies, bless those who curse you, do good to those who hate you, and pray for those who spitefully use you and persecute you.

Would our great Teacher tell us to do what He would not do? No, this prayer from the cross was absolutely consistent with what He taught us about praying for our persecutors.

Perhaps equally convincing proof that Jesus truly meant what He said in this prayer was the example of the martyr Stephen when he was being stoned to death by the same men who had condemned Jesus and demanded His death. Listen to these words from Acts 7: *And they stoned Stephen as he was calling on God and saying, Lord Jesus receive my spirit. Then he knelt down and cried out in a loud voice, Lord do not charge them with this sin.* This, I believe, is probably the surest example and explanation of the words of Jesus when He said: *Father, forgive them.*

In Isaiah 53 we read these prophetic words concerning the Messiah, *He bore the sins of many and made intercession for the transgressors.* What wondrous love is this, O my soul? In His intercession for the transgressors, our Lord asked for their forgiveness with added urgency when He said of them, *They know not what they do.* What amazing grace! What a reminder to us who always want to ascribe the worst of motives to those who do us wrong, with little if any room for grace in our hearts.

How was this request answered?

In God's amazing forbearance, the people of Jerusalem would have another generation of grace before the destruction of Jerusalem. During that time, thousands upon thousands would come to faith in the Lord Jesus as Messiah, and the church in Jerusalem would become one of the first centers of missionary activity for the Roman world. The light from some of the brightest stars in the Christian galaxy graced that city—not only the original Apostles, but Stephen and Barnabas, and of all people, Saul who became Paul the Apostle. In Acts *6:7,* we read these words: *Then the word of God spread, and the number of disciples multiplied greatly in Jerusalem, and a great many of the priests were obedient to the faith.* I believe all this was at least a part of the Father's answer to this prayer of His Son from the cross.

What may we learn from these words, and how do they meet one of our deepest needs?

If our Lord Jesus prayed such a prayer for those who were directly responsible for His suffering and death, what must be the power of His unceasing intercession for His precious elect whom the Father had given Him in the Covenant of Redemption from before the foundation of the world! I believe there are two great lessons we must learn from this, the first of the Jesus' last words from the cross:

A.   Satan often takes his deadly whip and attempts to scourge my guilty conscience with the taunts and fears he uses so effectively, and drives me to the point of hopeless despair by reminding me over and over again of all my sins which truly deserve death and hell. Then, above his strident accusations and their echoes within my own conscience, and even beyond the tormenting pain I feel, I may hear again from God's precious word my suffering Savior say: *Father, forgive them for they know not what they do.* And as Satan is rebuked by God's word, it is as though upon my lacerated back of conscience I feel the healing power of the tears and blood He shed for me. Then I know "There is a balm in Gilead that makes the wounded whole," and so may you.

B. The other issue is this: What right do I have to say of the slights, accusations, being ignored, hurt, the object of anger and spite, "That is unforgivable!" Yes, the hurt is real; it can cause much suffering of body, mind, and spirit; and it may wound my heart and damage my life. But I must remember the prayer of my Savior from the cross. *Father, forgive them for they do not know what they do.*

You may be protesting right now saying, "But you just don't understand how much I've been hurt." You're right of course, but does Jesus not know? Did He not understand how bad things could be when He said: *Love your enemies, bless those who curse you; do good to those who hate you, and pray for those who persecute you, and despitefully use you* Was He not serious when He said. So *will My heavenly Father also do to you if each of you, from his heart, does not forgive his brother's trespasses?* Can I claim to follow Him who prayed such a prayer and still refuse to obey this basic command?

But you may protest and explain away your unforgiving heart by putting all sorts of conditions on your willingness to forgive. When Jesus prayed: *Father, forgive them, for they know not what they do,* did He add, *but only if they meet my conditions, and agree with My definitions of what forgiveness means?*

Ask God to give you a forgiving spirit which will enable you to pray that they be forgiven as you have been forgiven by your Father in heaven. Then the prayer of the Lord Jesus from the cross will be answered in you.

2

"TODAY YOU WILL BE WITH ME IN PARADISE"

Matthew 20:1-16; Luke 23:32-43

And Jesus said, Assuredly I say to you,
today you will be with Me in paradise.

In many ways, this is the most remarkable of all the seven say-ings from Jesus on the cross, and once more it speaks to two of the most basic needs of the human heart: the need for belong-ing or community, and the longing for heaven. In another sense, this was a way for the Savior to express confidence that the Father had heard His prayer, *Father, forgive them,* for He knew that this man's sins had been forgiven.

We like to deny that we need anyone else, and we say we are self-sufficient, but we know that's not true. We need to belong. Sometimes that longing for heaven lies buried deep in our hearts, its voice stilled by the temporary pleasures of this world and its siren call, "It doesn't get any better than this."

Or maybe we're just too busy to think about heaven—or hell, for that matter. But in the stillness of the night when no one else is there, when even the television and the Internet have been turned off, there may come a deep sigh from within your soul that reminds you how fragile and temporary this life is. Perhaps when it becomes clear that you or your dearest one will soon face death, then like it or not, you must consider eternal things. That's what happened to a certain man long ago who realized his time had come and he had no claim on heaven or anything else but death and hell. We call that man the thief on the cross.

Three men were dying on crosses that day—two who were robbers and probably murderers as well, and another who had been accused of blasphemy, a crime of which all His accusers and the one who sentenced Him to die knew He was not guilty.

The two thieves

In their pain and anger, both of the robbers began to revile Jesus with the same angry, mocking words the chief priests, the scribes, the Pharisees and the elders were using in their abuse of Jesus. And what were these hypocritical religious leaders shouting out against the dying Jesus? Just listen: *You who destroy the temple and rebuild it in three days, save yourself. If you are the Son of God, come down from the cross. He saved others, He cannot save Himself. If He is the King of Israel, let Him down from the cross and we will believe Him. He trusted in God to deliver Him, let Him deliver Him if He delights in Him, for He said, I am the Son of God.*

As the pain increased in both these wretches being crucified with Jesus, the anger of one exploded into this blasphemy: *If You are the Messiah, save yourself and us!* But something had been happening to the other criminal. He grew silent, and when the first thief began to revile Jesus, the silent one rebuked his fellow criminal. He admitted his own guilt and said that both of them, the two criminals, were guilty and that their punishment was fully justified.

If you have ever spent much time around people who are in prison, you know that it is indeed a rare thing when a person owns responsibility for their punishment, and admits that justice has been done in his or her incarceration. But for a man who was in the midst of the cruelest form of execution possible to say, *we are being punished justly,* was a sure sign that his repentance was as real as his confession.

He went on to declare that Jesus had been unjustly condemned and was being unjustly punished. (Ironically, Pilate had said the same thing but still allowed His crucifixion.) Repentance led to faith, faith led to open confession of unworthiness, and confession ultimately led to a plea for forgiveness and cleansing.

What had happened to this man? How was such a change possible? I think it began when the horror of reality dawned in his soul. He had been tried by a court of law and condemned because he was guilty. Shortly he would face the ultimate Judge, and he knew that he was also guilty of breaking all the laws of God and thus deserved eternal death and hell. The fear of God fell upon him like a giant boulder and crushed him. The first evidence of this was his rebuke of his partner in crime. *Do you not even fear God, seeing you are under the same condemnation? And we indeed justly for we receive the due reward of our deeds. But this man has done nothing wrong.*

Then I think the first glimmer of hope dawned into his soul when he heard Jesus pray. *"Father, forgive them…."* If this man could ask God to forgive those who were guilty of unjustly killing Him for crimes He never committed, maybe He can forgive me for the crimes I have committed. He also had to notice that Jesus did not retaliate with words even though He could have justly denied all their false accusations. And he, like everyone else in Jerusalem and far beyond, had heard about this man and the miracles He performed, even raising the dead.

These factors were means God used in his conversion, but the real reason he changed was that God in His magnificent, sovereign grace had regenerated his dead heart. We can only conclude, that he, like us, had been chosen in Christ from before the foundation of the world, and so in God's way and God's time he came to saving faith.

The imperfect request of the dying thief

The thief's faith was still small and imperfect, but it was true and genuine. He knew that "Nothing in my hand I bring, simply to Thy cross I cling; naked come to Thee for dress, helpless look to Thee for grace; Foul I to the fountain fly, wash me Savior or I die." So he said, *Jesus, remember me when You come into Your kingdom.*

How much did this man really understand? Where did he get the idea that this man dying next to him on his own cross would have a kingdom into which a dying thief might enter?

The dying thief was almost certainly a Jew, and as such he would certainly have some knowledge of the Jews' expectations of a Messiah and a grand Messianic kingdom at the end of the age. He also seemed to know something about Jesus, His life and ministry, for he said of Him, *This man has done nothing wrong.*

There is something about this man's humble petition which reminds me of the words spoken by the Syro-Phoencian woman who came to Jesus seeking help for her demon-possessed daughter. Jesus told her, *It is not right to take the children's food and feed it to the dogs under the table.* Her response of humility and faith was simply this: *Yes, Lord, but even the little dogs eat the crumbs which fall from their Master's table.* Those words earned from Jesus a glowing commendation for her faith—and the healing of her daughter.

Now here this dying thief expresses an even greater faith in Jesus than the woman's. He was not asking what James and John had asked for themselves—the highest place of honor in the kingdom. He knew he was not worthy of any place of honor or even a place. He knew he was a sinner with no claim on Jesus or His kingdom. But he also knew the very name Jesus, meant Savior and as such an heir to David's throne.

These may have been the last coherent words this man was ever able to speak. Soon the pain would overwhelm him, and then at the very last they would come and break his legs so he could no longer push himself up to catch a breath. But while a spark of life and sanity still remained, he called upon Jesus.

Perhaps someone who reads this message today is feeling in despair. Maybe you realize that so much of your life is now past and still you are unsure of your salvation. Please, from within your heart while life and breath remain, call out to Him who gave His life a ransom for many, *Jesus, remember me when you come in your kingdom.*

The perfect response of the Lord Jesus

Assuredly I say to you, today, you will be with me in Paradise. Jesus' response assured the repentant thief that he would abide in His presence forever. The Lord offered this man abundantly above what he asked or could possibly think. This dying man asked for entrance into a kingdom one day, a kingdom he did not understand but that he hoped existed somewhere in the far-distant future of eternity. But Jesus said to him. *Today you will be with me in paradise.* The thief would not live to see the sun set on this day, but before the day was over, he would be with Jesus in His blessed kingdom.

How many of us understand that today is the day of salvation? Eternal life begins when you come to the Lord and call upon His grace. You don't have to wait until some vague uncertain day or time in the by-and-by. Salvation, assurance, peace— these gifts may be yours even now, for the gift of God which is eternal life brings with it the fullness of God's pardoning love, and acceptance now and forever.

The thief had asked, *Lord, remember me when You come into Your kingdom.* Jesus answered. *You will be with Me.* To be absent from the body is to be present with the Lord. He will acknowledge you before the Father, and where He is, there will you be also.

The story is told of a young king who tried valiantly but vainly to defend his small kingdom against invading Roman legions. After he was captured, he and his wife were brought before Caesar who was afield with his triumphant army. The young king's valor was not honored, and he and his wife were sentenced to die immediately. The distraught young man fell down before Caesar and pled for him to spare his wife, saying, "Only I lifted my sword against you. Let me die for us both, but please release her to return to her family and home."

With many tears and pleas he begged for her life, offering over and over again to die in her place. Finally Caesar was moved by his unselfish courage. He summoned the defeated king and his wife to stand before him and granted them full pardon and released them to return home upon condition of faithfulness to Caesar.

As they walked away rejoicing in Caesar's mercy, the young man said to his wife, "Did you see how magnificent Caesar was?"

"No," she replied. "I only had eyes to see the man who was willing to die for me." For all eternity, I believe we will have eyes only for the One who died in our place.

The thief asked to be remembered when Jesus came into His kingdom, but Jesus answered, *Today you will be with Me in paradise.* Let the scholars debate what Jesus meant by the word paradise, but in the context it can have but one meaning: heaven. There are several places in Scripture in which the words heaven and paradise are used interchangeably.

If by grace-granted faith you look to the Lord Jesus Christ and know He died on the cross in your place, you may call upon Him for mercy even as the thief of old called upon Him. Grace, pardon, and salvation you will be granted, but so much more than your mind can possibly conceive. From the moment of that feeble cry, and for all eternity, you will belong to Him and inherit the kingdom prepared for you from before the foundation of the world.

3

"LOOK! YOUR SON...
LOOK, YOUR MOTHER..."

John 19:17-27

Of all the Lord's words spoken from the cross, these to His mother and to His best friend John are the most poignant and in some ways the most endearing. Yet if we dwell upon this only or even primarily as an expression of a son's loving concern for His mother, I think we will miss much of the importance and power of what He said.

Having said that, we must recognize that one aspect of this exchange is Jesus' active obedience to the fifth commandment. In fact, obedience to each of the commandments may be discerned in His seven last words from the cross.

These words to John and Mary involve so many things. They speak of duty to parents and of concern for dear friends. They speak of compassion for those who suffer, and of a desire to somehow mitigate that suffering. They also speak of relationships and duties beyond our immediate family, and to the recognition that we are members of a much larger and enduring family of faith in Jesus Christ.

No, being a Christian does not negate our obligations to family, it just enlarges the circle of responsibility, and intensifies the reality of duty we have for both our birth family and our faith family.

Jesus and Mary

There had always been a very special bond between Jesus and His mother. It began with the supernatural conception of the pre-natal Jesus within the womb of the virgin Mary.

I have an idea that there were only three people in the world who knew the true story of Jesus' conception: Mary, Joseph, and Mary's cousin Elizabeth. Of course add to that number one more, Jesus Himself. Mary and her husband Joseph would have several other children, but with Jesus it would have been different: not only was He the firstborn, but He alone was the virgin-born.

It was to Mary that Simeon spoke when Joseph and Mary took the infant boy to the temple for the rite of purification. After thanking God for fulfilling His promise that he (Simeon) would not die until he had seen the Messiah, he warned Mary that a sword would break her heart because of her Son.

Later when Jesus went to the temple as a young lad, presumably to celebrate His bar-mitzvah. He became separated from His parents for three days. When after a frantic search they found him discussing theology with the temple rabbis, Mary rebuked Him for causing His parents such anxiety. Jesus' surprised response was, *But did you not know that I must be in My Father's house and about My Father's business?* Still, He went home and submitted to His parents' authority.

Even in this incident there is an indication that Jesus understood that He had a higher calling beyond family loyalty, and that He placed duty to His Father above even His responsibility to His parents. His obedient response to them, however, was a part of His higher duty to "be about His Father's business."

What about the relationship between Jesus and Mary? After Jesus began His public ministry, there is an indication that He recognized that Mary would have to adjust to a new kind of relationship in which He would no longer defer to her will and wishes in all things. As a child under the authority of His parents, Jesus recognized their role of authority over Him, which according to Luke 3:51, He readily accepted: *And He went down with them and came to Nazareth and was submissive to them.* But from the beginning of His public ministry, Mary struggled with the idea that Jesus was no longer under her roof or under her authority.

If you are a parent of grown children, you will understand something of her ongoing struggle. You have to be there for them when and if they need you and ask for your help, but you no longer have a role of authority and control over their lives.

Let me say this gently, but I hope you will hear it well. All too often I have seen the conscious or at best unconscious efforts of parents to control the lives of their grown children and children-in-law. For instance, too often what happens in wedding ceremonies does not reflect the wishes of the bride but of her mother. I know you think that's kind of funny and almost inevitable, but really it is neither. Especially in small towns and rural congregations, many young couples are not free to plan their own holidays or even Sunday dinners because of parental and or grandparental pressure to conform to long-standing customs which are held to be inviolable.

Two incidents leading up to the cross helped prepare Mary for the words she would hear from her dying Son: the wedding in Cana of Galilee and the episode in which Mary brought all the other children with her to the place where Jesus was staying in an apparent attempt to take Him home and "straighten Him out."

At the Cana wedding reception, the host found himself in the embarrassing situation of having run out of wine to serve the guests. When this became known to Mary, who was probably a friend of the family or perhaps a co-hostess, she called upon Jesus, presumably to get Him to do something about the situation. I have no idea what her expectations were, but obviously she felt she was within her rights to help direct Jesus in His ministry.

His response was respectful but clearly rejected Mary's effort to direct Him to her ends. When she said, *They have run out of wine.* His response was, *Woman, what does this have to do with Me? My hour has not yet come.* He did not address her as "mother." By addressing her as "woman," He was using a title of respect, but nevertheless He was telling her that His ministry direction could not come from her, as He must be about His Father's business. It was necessary for Mary's sake that a radical change in the relationship must occur. Sooner or later, she would have to confess Jesus as her Lord and Savior, but the time was not yet ripe for this change. That He proceeded to perform one of His first miracles in response to the need of the moment was not because of Mary's implied request, but because He chose this time to manifest the glory of who He was and to begin a work of faith in His disciples.

The second incident is almost shocking in that it demonstrated Mary's failure to learn the lesson Jesus was trying to teach her, and that she still thought only in human terms about their relationship. Her attitude was almost shocking in light of all she had been told about her Son by the angel Gabriel. Had she forgotten about the witness of the Shepherds and the wise men, who came to adore and worship Him as an infant? Had she forgotten that Gabriel told her, *He shall be great, and will be called the Son of the Highest, and the Lord God will give Him the throne of His Father David, and He will reign over the house of Jacob forever, and of His kingdom there shall be no end?* Now, here comes Mary with the rest of the family seeking Jesus, presumably with the idea of rebuking Him for His teaching and taking Him home. At least we know from John that His earthly brothers did not believe on Him, until after His resurrection.

So far as we know, on this occasion Jesus did not even talk with His earthly family, although they may have overheard what He said to those around Him. I must assume that they either heard or the messenger they sent in to get Jesus returned and told them what He said. And what did He say?

Listen to these words from Mark: *And His mother and His brothers came, and standing outside, they sent to Him and called Him. And a crowd was sitting around Him and they said to Him, Your mother and brothers are outside seeking You. And He answered them, Who are my mother and My brothers? And looking about at those who sat around Him, He said, Here are my mother and My brothers! Whoever does the will of God, he is My brother and sister and mother.*

By these words, Jesus elevated the spiritual relationship to Him above any earthly claims of kith and kin. Without faith in Him as Lord and Savior, none of Jesus' earthly family was truly His kin. He was not repudiating His family; He was saying that in the kingdom, spiritual kinship takes priority over earthly claims. How joyful the Lord's heart must have been when His earthly family joined His heavenly family by acknowledging Him as Savior and Lord.

The words of Jesus to Mary from His cross

Now we come to this truly poignant scene at the cross, for Mary was there. A sharp sword, in the form of bitter nails and a bloodstained cross, was breaking her heart. Surely her grief was adding to His, for He understood what pain she was enduring. And I believe the Savior knows and cares for each grief we experience. *For we do not have a High Priest who is unable to sympathize with our weaknesses, but one who in every respect has been tempted as we are.* So Mary's great grief became His grief—and so has yours. The Lord Jesus was actually doing the greatest thing He would ever do for Mary in dying on the cross to save her from her sins. But He also would fulfill His duty to her as her firstborn Son, for in the traditions of the time it was the firstborn son's responsibility to care for parents in need.

But why didn't He at least call her *Mother?* I think his words to Mary, including calling her *Woman,* was motivated not only by duty but even more by compassion. Mary needed to understand that the death of Jesus was so much more than just a son dying in the presence of a beloved mother.

The first time He addressed her as *Woman,* at Cana, He was drawing a line of demarcation in their relationship but went on to perform a miracle for her benefit and for the benefit of many others. Now, the second time He called her *Woman,* He was performing a far greater miracle for her benefit and for a vast host of others, accepting her punishment and yours and mine that we might truly become the children of God.

Mary would not have completely understood all that was happening or even the full import of His words to her until after His resurrection, when she could look back and see the love and tender kindness Jesus demonstrated to her. She would also see that His suffering on her behalf and that of so many more was God's way of bringing her into everlasting joy.

She would also have a loving "son," John—Jesus' best friend—who was so much like the Son she gave up and who would tenderly care for her the rest of her life. And one day, John would come with her before the throne and worship the great Lamb of God and Lion of Judah, her Lord and her God.

One final lesson I learn from these words of Jesus to Mary: He has infinite love and compassion for all His beloved elect whom the Father had given Him. There are times when I do

not understand what is happening in my life any more than
Mary at first could make sense of what appeared to be the ultimate tragedy of her Son being taken away just as His life
seemed to be getting under way. But in the end, I will be able
to look back on all that has happened in my life and affirm that
God works all things together for good to those who love the
Lord, to those who are called according to His purpose,
because He died for me and rose again.

4

THE CRY FROM A BROKEN HEART

Psalm 22; Mark 15:34

When our Lord Jesus Christ was dying in pain and anguish on the dreadful cross, He experienced all the agonies of a soul in hell. His physical pain was well nigh unbearable, the mental anguish was unimaginable, and the spiritual pain was beyond comprehending. The pain increased as the hours wore on, and the darkness in His soul was reflected in the strange and horrible mid-day darkness which filled the land. Not since the days of the plagues on Egypt had such darkness been seen or felt. Finally, just before the end, something was added more awful than all the other pain of body, mind and spirit He had endured: He had to experience the terrible wrath of God His Father, when He who knew no sin became sin for us. All the evil and all the sins committed from the day Adam fell in

Eden's garden to the end of the world, all the misery of sin's consequences was heaped on Him. God, the holy One, dealt with His beloved Son just as if He had been guilty of all these things and as if He deserved the flames of hell.

Up to that point, our blessed Savior had uttered few words. He had committed His mother to the care of faithful John, He had asked the Father to forgive those who crucified Him, He had promised the thief he would be with Him that very day in God's blessed paradise, and He had groaned that He was thirsty. But then when His soul was made an offering for sin and all our sins were transferred to His account and laid upon His heart, it was too much. He who had dwelt from all eternity in the presence of the Father in perfect unity suddenly found Himself abandoned and cursed, the object of holy wrath.

Then from His broken and crushed heart and from His thirsty lips there came that awful cry of deepest anguish. *My God, My God, why have You forsaken me?* These words were but the beginning of a Psalm of David which the Lord knew from His heart. Other words from this same Psalm were used by Jesus' enemies while He was hanging on the cross. *He trusted in the Lord, let Him rescue Him; Let Him deliver Him if He delights in Him.* Some of the words of this Psalm describe very graphically the physical sufferings of the One who was crucified. *I am poured out like water, and all my bones are out of joint; My heart is like wax; it has melted within me. My strength is dried up like a potsherd, and My tongue cleaves to my jaws. You have brought Me to the dust of death. They pierced my hands ands my feet; I can count my bones. They divided my garments among them, and for my clothing they cast lots.*

The sufferings of David

This Psalm was written a thousand years before Jesus was crucified. How are we to understand the connection? Did David have a mystic vision that spanned a thousand years to see his holy Descendent dying on the cross, and so write these words? No, the Holy Spirit was speaking through David of things which David had experienced to a small degree and described poetically. But He was also speaking through David of things far beyond David's experience or knowledge.

Allowing for poetic exaggeration, David had indeed gone through much disappointment and suffering at many times in his life. As a young lad he was mocked and taunted by his older brothers, especially when he volunteered to do what they feared to do—face Goliath in battle. Then after his great victory over the giant, King Saul became jealous of him, and David had to flee for his life. In his own words, he was but one step from death, surrounded in the wilderness by Saul's warriors and with little hope of escape. After his disastrous affair with Bathsheba, he suffered great mental and spiritual anguish because of the dreadful weight of sin which rested on his heart. Even after being forgiven, the consequences of his sins continued to bear bitter fruit. His daughter was violated by her own half-brother, and he in turn was murdered by angry Absalom. This young man then turned against his father David and led a rebellion in which he sought to disgrace, dethrone and kill David. Still David loved him, and when Absalom was killed, David's heart was broken.

So the anguish described in Psalm 22, though not fully a description of David's suffering, was still apropos to his life.

We too may be called upon to suffer many things in our own lives and in the lives of those we love. There are times when we may even feel forsaken by God, but nothing can separate us as believers from Him permanently. We may suffer disgrace, intense physical pain, deep disappointment in ourselves and others, mental and spiritual anguish, and perplexing confusion. Most painful of all is the feeling that God has abandoned us.

The sufferings of Jesus upon the cross

The Holy Spirit who guided the mind and words of the writer knew that this poetical description of David's suffering would be the actual, literal experience of Jesus Christ when He was crucified. Most of His friends had forsaken Him, and His enemies surrounded Him and taunted Him in His great agony. They ridiculed Him and mocked Him with these words: *He trusted in God; let Him deliver Him now if He will have Him, for He said, 'I am the Son of God.'* They added, *He saved others, Himself He cannot save. If He is the King of Israel, let Him come down from the cross. Then,* they lied, *"we will believe in Him."*

Like wild and bellowing bulls they yelled at Him and mocked His pain and agony. After this they would hurry to the Temple to prepare for the Passover feast, the most holy day of all; for after all, they were the religious leaders, the holy men of their people.

It is astounding that David's figurative language could describe so graphically what actually happened to Jesus on the cross. Such words as *I am poured out like water and all my bones are out of joint"* describe what really happened to those being crucified. *My heart has melted within me* may well anticipate what some medical experts say happened to Jesus, that His heart ruptured as the immediate and medical cause of death. Other expressions as *My tongue cleaves to my jaws ... they pierced my hands and my feet ... they divided my garments among them and for my robe they cast lots ...* sound more like a reporter on the scene than a prophet long years before Jesus died.

Why was all this written and fulfilled? There are several reasons and one above all others.

1. These things were written that we might see something of the amazing nature of God's Holy Word. Every word is true and all are fulfilled.

2. God's mysterious sovereignty and providence is clearly shown forth. In all these things we see the plan and purpose of God being worked out. Each and every detail of His plan of salvation was known of Him from before the foundation of the world. When Peter preached his great sermon at Pentecost, he said exactly this: *Jesus was delivered by the determined purpose and foreknowledge of God, and you with wicked hands have crucified and put Him to death.*

3. They were written and fulfilled so that we might fully appreciate all it cost God and His Son to forgive our sins and so that we might have the honor and blessing of belonging to Him.

4. For the last and most important reason of all, we have but to look at the last half of this Psalm. Here we discover the reason above all others: His sacrifice availed! The Savior's terrible suffering was soon over, but the blessed results endure forever. *All the ends of the earth shall remember and turn to the Lord, and all the families of the nations shall worship before You. For the kingdom is the Lord's and He rules*

over the nations....They will come and declare His
righteousness to a people who will be born, that He has done
this. So after the Savior's heart-broken cry as He endured
God's holy wrath and displeasure, the sacrifice was complete.
He cried, *It is finished. Father, into Your hands I commend My*
spirit, and He died. Then the veil of the temple was torn in
two from top to bottom, and the way into the Holiest of
Holies was opened forever.

And so we come to that holy place. There is no longer an altar
of sacrifice or a need for one. Instead there is a simple table
spread with bread and the fruit of the vine, but this table is far
more holy than even that ancient altar and the meal we eat
together is far more effective for the cleansing of sin. Come,
aware of your Savior's sacrifice, His pain, His grief and above
all His final victory over sin—*your* sin.

5

"I Thirst."

Psalm 42; John 19:25-30

The agony of the cross was almost over. Jesus had spoken four times since the crucifixion began. The recorded words of Jesus when He reached the very depths of His suffering, when He as the sin-bearer—the Lamb of God who takes away the sins of the world—endured the wrath and curse of God upon sin and cried out, *My God, My God, why have you forsaken Me?* This helps us understand more fully His next three sayings and especially the one that immediately followed this heart-broken cry.

The Lord Jesus had endured hunger and burning thirst while He was being tempted in the wilderness at the very beginning of His earthly ministry, but the thirst He endured upon the cross was even more severe physically and spiritually than anything He had ever endured before. His last food and drink had been the Passover meal the night before. His last sleep had been Wednesday night, if then, and by the time this word of thirst was uttered He was probably burning up with fever, dehydration, and loss of blood. So He cried in deep agony, *I thirst.*

But I think there was more to this word than the physical suffering He endured; I believe there was a spiritual thirst burning within Him too. He had just passed through the deepest suffering imaginable, when total separation from the Father had wrung from His lips and inmost being the bitter cry of One forsaken. As you have heard me say before, this is why we say with wonder and reverence in the words of the Apostles' Creed, "He descended into Hell." Is there a more miserable, devastating experience in all the world than feeling yourself cut off from God? God never forsakes His own, but there are many times when His own feel utterly forsaken and spiritually destitute. And at times we justly feel this agony of separation as we remember the words of Isaiah to Israel, *Your sins have separated you from God.*

Now stop and consider that He was and forever is God's only begotten Son, in whom the Father is well pleased. But when His soul was made an offering for sin. He was cut off from the Father, and there was total darkness in His soul. It was not that Jesus *felt* forsaken—He *was* forsaken, and even worse He was accounted as guilty of all your sins and mine too! I think, therefore, that this word, I *thirst,* was a heart-cry at the deepest level for this separation that caused a spiritual thirst beyond imagination to end, and for the Father's face to shine upon Him once more.

Perhaps this word from the lips of our dying Lord was all of Psalm 42 that He was physically able to utter. In God's providence and under the inspiration of the Holy Spirit, the agony David experienced to a much lesser degree and which he described in this psalm, seems to have been written just for the spiritual agony of Jesus on the cross. Listen again: *My soul thirsts for God, for the living God. When shall I come and appear before God? My tears have been My food day and night, while they continually say to Me, where is your God?*

The suffering of the Lord Jesus during His life and ministry

But at the same time, the physical side of His suffering was all too real. In fact, the story of His incarnation and His short life is a story of unbelievable suffering. C.S. Lewis once said that when God the Son became a man, it was a much further step down for Him than if a man became a snail or slug. Lewis went on the say that we share creaturehood with the lowest forms of life because we are both created, but for the Creator to become also a creature was unthinkable—except that it really happened.

He was born of lowly parentage, and who besides Joseph and Elizabeth believed Mary's story of how Jesus was conceived? When He was a tiny boy. His parents had to flee into Egypt to save His life. Upon their return, they settled in Nazareth where Jesus grew up as the son of Joseph the Carpenter. That would not mean abject poverty, but it would mean the level of the peasant population. After His public ministry began, He truly lived a life of privation. The first 40 days were spent in the southern Judean desert wilderness being tempted of the devil and fasting for over one long month. Shortly thereafter, a certain scribe came to Him and said he wanted to follow Jesus wherever He would go. His reply was a summary of those three years before His passion and death: *Foxes have holes, and birds of the air have nests, but the Son of Man has nowhere to lay His head.*

That remained true throughout His short life, and when He was dead they even placed His dear body in a borrowed tomb. He was deprived of family, a permanent home, and a settled life. His travels were all on foot except for an occasional ride in a little fishing boat. When he entered the city to offer Himself as the true Messiah, He had to borrow a donkey to ride on. His meager livelihood apparently depended upon whatever contributions some would give Him and His disciples to sustain themselves.

There was another side to His earthly life of privation and want: many simply hated Him without cause except for the fact that He exposed their own shallowness and hypocrisy. His circle of friends was very small, and even His best friends were unreliable when the pinch came. Many for whom He performed mighty miracles of grace and healing cared little for His teaching. All His life He "thirsted" and had so little of all the things we take for granted. Really, no one was capable of understanding Him on a human level.

The experience in the Garden of Gethsemane

It is ironic that what led Him into His dreadful "thirst" on the cross was His willingness to drink the cup the Father gave Him. This sounds like a contradiction, but it isn't if you think it through. I doubt that He experienced physical thirst in the garden, as He and the disciples had eaten the Passover meal a short time earlier. But if you think of thirst in terms of isolation, it was truly a burning thirst of spirit. He asked His disciples to watch and pray with Him as He went before the Father to wrestle with the dreadful decision which lay immediately before Him. He even took His "inner circle"—Peter, James, and John—apart from the others so that they might support and comfort Him in His hour of grief. But what happened? Even these faithful three proved unfaithful in His time of need. After the first spiritual battle, He came back to them, weary and weeping, I think, and said, *What? Could you not watch and pray with Me one hour?* Then He returned to face the unbearable again, and once more while He wrestled long in tears and groaning, they slept.

Just what did Jesus mean when He prayed, O *My Father, take this cup from Me?* And again: *If this cup cannot pass from Me except I drink it, Thy will be done.* He was referring to the cross and the pain and shame which faced Him there. He was trying to come to grips with the terrible trauma of suffering the wrath and curse of God against sin, though He Himself was sinless. That experience would be far worse than even the dreadful anticipation which nearly consumed His mind and heart as He prayed there in the garden.

There are times when our fears of an approaching event are worse than the event itself (except for a root canal), but in this case no fear or dread could match the awfulness of what He would go through on the cross. I say again, it was His willingness to drink the cup which made Him so utterly thirsty as He hung on the cross.

The suffering of Christ on the cross before He uttered this word

Christ's suffering on the cross was brutal and indescribable. The intensity of that suffering increased each moment and hour He was there. It is not my purpose to dwell on the physical side of His ordeal, but neither can we ignore it in our effort to understand this fifth saying of Jesus. His suffering is handled with a degree of reserve in the Gospel accounts so that we would dwell not on what He went through, but on what He accomplished.

His physical suffering was real and horrible. There is nothing about any of our experiences in this world which would prepare us to even faintly imagine the cruelty of crucifixion. One might ask, "Why did the Gospel writers go into any detail at all?" The answer is that even in the first few decades of the church there were false teachers who tried to convince people that Jesus was not really a man at all but only appeared to be, and that He did not die on the cross. This teaching was tearing the heart out of the Gospel, and some fell for it. The Apostles who wrote the four Gospels saw clearly the need to establish the death of Jesus as a reality. What better way to prove His true humanity than to describe His actual suffering and death? John even went so far as to describe in some detail what happens to human blood when one dies.

But in our Lord's case, the spiritual suffering was far more deadly. The weight of the sins of the world—from Adam until the last living person on earth draws his last breath—was laid on Jesus. We cannot even bear the weight of our own sinful hearts, but Jesus the sinless One became, as it were, Jesus the vilest sinner who ever lived. So there was wrung from Him the cry of the forsaken, and then the cry of a thirst too deep and searing to describe.

During His ministry, the Lord Jesus offered the unfailing water of life on at least two occasions.

In John 4, we read the story of Jesus and the woman at the well in Samaria. I won't go into the whole story, but only the offer Jesus made to her: *If you knew the gift of God, and who it is who says to you, give me a drink, you would have asked Him, and He would have given you living water. Whoever drinks of the water that I shall give him will never thirst. But the water I give him will become a fountain of water springing up into everlasting life.* He saved others from this deadly thirst, but in order to do so, He could not and would not save Himself.

Jesus offered the water of life to the thirsty on another occasion, the Feast of Tabernacles. Among other things, this feast celebrated God's miraculous provisions for Israel in the wilderness, and especially the water flowing from the rock at Meribah. This feast not only commemorated that past event; it also anticipated the outpouring of God's grace on Israel and the whole world. The celebration culminated when the priests drew water from the pool of Siloam and poured it out to remind the people of how God had brought water from the rock, accompanied by fervent prayers for the coming of the Messianic kingdom. At that dramatic moment, Jesus stepped forward and cried out with a loud voice, *If anyone is thirsty; let him come to Me and drink.* There could be no clearer proof that Jesus was offering Himself as the Messiah who would bring blessing upon Israel and upon the whole world. But again. He could only make this amazing offer because on the cross He would cry out, *I thirst.*

His word of grace still stands. He offers the water of life to cleanse our guilty souls, and He offers the water of grace to satisfy our deepest longings for peace and joy. These gifts are ours to claim by faith.

The formula is simple yet deeply profound. Accept His offer by obeying Him when He said, *Repent and believe, for the kingdom of heaven is at hand.* Let this be the song of our hearts:

> *I heard the voice of Jesus say,*
> *Behold I freely give*
> *the living water, thirsty one.*
> *Stoop down and drink and live.*
> *I came to Jesus and I drank of that life-giving*
>   *stream!*
> *My thirst was quenched, my soul revived, and*
>   *now I live in Him.*
>   *(Horatius Bonar)*

Come. Drink and live!

6

"It Is Finished."

Revelation 21:1-8; John 19:28-37

Jesus' strength was failing rapidly. The pain and agony of all
that had happened to Him, beginning with His prayer of final
surrender to the Father's will in Gethsemane, had brought Him
to the very brink of death. But before the end there were yet
two more words He would speak: *It is finished,* and *Father, into
Your hands I commend My spirit.* It is upon these words, *It is
finished, we* now focus our attention.

This statement is much more than awareness of approaching
death. Listen again to these words: *After this, Jesus, knowing
that all things were now accomplished, that the Scripture might
be fulfilled, said, I thirst.* His next words were *It is finished!* If
we are to understand what He meant by that, we have to inter-
pret the word *finished* by these two previous words, *accomplished and fulfilled.*

I think there is a very real sense in which Jesus was referring to the entire meaning of His incarnation and the purpose for which He left heaven to enter this sin-cursed world. It would be a terrible mistake to think of these words as words of defeat, or even surrender to death. It was not as if Jesus was saying, *I tried my best but it's over now.* It is not as if He was saying what Elijah said under the juniper bush, totally defeated by life and by the wicked power of Ahab and Jezebel: *It is enough, now take away my life, O Lord, for I am not better than my fathers.*

These are incredible words of an accomplishment so great as to be beyond our understanding. Contrary to all outward appearances, contrary to what the gloating enemies thought, contrary to even the heartbroken despair of His defeated disciples, He had fulfilled and accomplished all the Father had given Him to do. He had defeated death, hell and the devil. And only the triune God—Father, Son, and Holy Spirit—knew what He had accomplished even at the very moment of His death and because of His birth, life and death.

The only thing that seemed "finished" to the outward eye was Jesus Himself. He had preached, healed, taught, loved and lived out a complete obedience to the two great commandments of which He said, *On these two commandments hang all the law and the prophets.* Those two commandments? Love God with all your heart, mind and strength, and love your neighbor as yourself. This He had done to absolute perfection, but that all seemed to be over now. He has been rejected, tried, condemned and executed, and with almost His last breath He said: *It is finished!*

How then can we begin to understand this as a great cry of victorious success in what He had been sent into the world to accomplish?

Several sayings of Jesus before the cross help us to rightly understand His next-to-last word from the cross. Let's review several so we may have complete and unshaken confidence today in the victory Jesus announced with these words: *It is finished!*

The world/life view of Jesus during His earthly ministry, as seen in several quotations from His words

A brief summary of this is His own statement: *I have not come to do My own will, but the will of Him who sent Me.* The entire meaning of His life is wrapped up in these words. In the final analysis, this is also the only thing which will give our lives significance and meaning.

If Jesus had lived to satisfy Himself, He would not have endured all He went through between His conception and His death. In fact, He would never have left His Father's side to begin with! Most certainly He would have lived an entirely different life than the one we discover in the Gospels, and He never would have said: *The Son of Man came not to be ministered unto but to minister, and to give His life a ransom for many.*

Jesus had every opportunity to be the most powerful, popular figure in Israel's history. Everyone was looking for a Messiah, and He was wildly popular during His early days of ministry. The common people were hugely impressed that Jesus was not cowed by the corrupt religious establishment, and they knew He had miraculous powers beyond any prophet in the nation's long history. The news of His healing the sick, His opening the eyes of the blind, and His unstopping the ears of the deaf spread like wildfire, and then before their very eyes He took a few morsels of bread and fish and fed the multitudes on two different occasions. The multitudes were determined to make Him king, by force if necessary, and then—as if that were not enough—He raised the dead! Even the rulers who feared and despised Him had to admit that a mighty miracle had taken place.

Let's face it: Jesus had it made. All He really needed to do was go to the top pinnacle of the temple and cast Himself down before the assembled multitudes who had come to the Passover Feast. Then even the reluctant and unbelieving rulers would not be able to deny His claim to be the Son of God, the Savior and King of Israel.

There was one problem. He had not come down from heaven to do His own will but the will of the Father who sent Him, and it was the Father's will that His Son be the sacrificial Lamb of God who would take away the sins of all those whom He had given to the Son from before the foundations of the world. It was the Father's will that Jesus would be the Good Shepherd who would lay down His life for the sheep.

The words which Jesus spoke during the passion week

Many of His words during that final week support the concept that Jesus by His death had accomplished the will of God, but only two need be set forth to prove the point: words about Him at the beginning of the Passover meal with His disciples, and the words of His great high-priestly prayer.

We read these words in John 13: *Now before the feast of the Passover, when Jesus knew that His hour had come that He should depart out of this world to the Father, having loved His own who were in the world. He loved them to the end. . . .Jesus knowing that the Father had given all things into His hands, and that He had come from God and was going (back) to God.*

The path from the last supper to the cross and to these almost final words of Jesus was one He walked intentionally, with His eyes open to all that would transpire. He had set out on a mission to save His sheep, and He knew it included His death on the cross. So as death was now at hand. He was able to say, *I have done what the Father sent Me to do.* The Good Shepherd had laid down His life for the sheep.

The words of Jesus in His high-priestly prayer add further proof to our understanding that when He said, *It is finished,* He was affirming success in His mission and victory over His enemies, especially Satan himself. Speaking to the Father, Jesus said *I have glorified You on earth. I have finished the work You gave Me to do.* Those words spoken just before He went to the cross anticipated the victory He would win. And now from the cross, He affirmed this triumph: *It is finished.*

The final, full explanation of *It is finished.*

There is only one way to finally and fully understand what Jesus meant when He said, *It is finished!* In Revelation 22, we read: *Then He that sat upon the throne said, Behold I make all things new. And He said to me, Write, for these words are true and faithful. And He said to me, It is done! I am Alpha and Omega, the Beginning and the End. I will give of the fountain of the water of life freely to him who thirsts. He who overcomes shall inherit all things, and I will be His God, and he shall be My son.*

Our Lord knew that upon His enthronement as King of kings and Lord of lords over the new heavens and the new earth, He would have completed the entire master plan of salvation determined in the Covenant of Redemption.

But for each individual person, one more step is needed. In the words of an old gospel song from long ago comes this claim of confident faith: *'Tis done, the great transaction's done, I am the Lord's and He is mine. (Philip Doddridge)*

That step is a step of faith, an act of surrender of your personal will to the will of the same Father to whom Jesus surrendered Himself in the Garden of Gethsemane.

The work of Jesus on your behalf is completed in one sense when by faith you claim Him as Lord and Savior. In another sense, this work will not be finished until you are made perfect in holiness and have been conformed to His own glorious image. Then you may say, "I am home at last. It is finished!"

7

"FATHER, INTO THY HANDS I COMMEND MY SPIRIT."

Luke 23:44-49

Hear once more all seven words our Lord Jesus spoke in His agony upon the cross. How beautifully they all tie together in perfect order. How fully they sum up the entire life, ministry and purpose of our Lord. How thoroughly they speak to every human need. How well they demonstrate our Lord's obedience to the two great commandments as summed up in Jesus' own words. How fittingly they demonstrate the entire meaning of all the other words He had spoken during the three years of His earthly ministry. Hear them one more time, in order:

1. Father, forgive them for they do not know what they are doing.

2. Assuredly I say to you, today you will be with Me in paradise.

3. Woman, look, your son! Look, your mother!

4. My God, My God, why have You forsaken Me?

5. I thirst.

6. It is finished.

7. Father, into Your hands I commend My spirit.

Do you see how it was impossible for Jesus to utter this last saying until He had said the previous six?

What do we hear in these words? We hear the very heart of Jesus. We hear forgiveness, grace and mercy. We hear compassion and care. We hear sacrifice, heartbreak and the deepest agony. We hear suffering and longing. We hear of incredible accomplishment, and finally we hear unlimited surrender to and complete confidence in the Father. What we hear is our own salvation being forever assured in a poignant, brilliant exposition of the word love—*agape* love.

Now let us hear with understanding and appreciation that final word from the cross, a word of total surrender and total trust.

The previous assertion and promise as found in John 10

In this chapter of John's Gospel, Jesus identified Himself as the Good Shepherd. It was then that Jesus predicted His own death, saying *I am the Good Shepherd. The Good Shepherd gives His life for the sheep.*

There are two things you must hear and understand from these words. The first is that Jesus was making it very clear that He would die only for His sheep. Later, He would identify His sheep as those whom the Father had given Him out of the world. If ever a passage of Scripture taught definitive atonement, it is this one. Salvation is a personal transaction between the Father and the Son on behalf of those called and chosen in Christ from before the foundation of the world.

Many well-meaning people think they honor God by proclaiming that Jesus died for everyone. No one with any understanding of God's immense power and love would ever deny that the Lord *could* have died for all people everywhere and in all ages, but no one who takes the words of the Lord Jesus seriously will stretch His claim beyond what He clearly reveals concerning His intentions.

Only a sentence or two later, the Lord added these words: *I know My sheep, and I am known by My own. As the Father knows Me, even so I know the Father, and I lay down My life for the sheep.* The implications of these words are very clear. The Father and the Son are in perfect agreement in knowing who His sheep are, and that He (Jesus) would very specifically and personally die for them alone.

The second thing to consider is the way in which the Lord referred to His death: *The Good Shepherd gives His life for the sheep.* Then He added: *Therefore My Father loves Me because I lay down My life that I may take it again. No one takes My life from Me, but I lay it down of Myself. I have power to lay it down, and I have power to take it again. This command I have received from My Father.*

Beloved, these are incredible, saving words! So we hear Jesus saying His last word from the cross: *Father, into Thy hands I commend My spirit.* As Luke notes, He said this with a loud voice, and we begin to understand something of the power of those words.

Jesus did not lose control at the very end and die at the hands of sinful mankind. Instead, He took control even of His own life and death. He gave Himself up fully to the Father for His beloved sheep of which you are one if you trust Him alone for salvation as He is offered in the Gospel.

All of the Gospel accounts of Jesus' death make it very clear that in a sacrificial act of accepting and drinking the cup of wrath the Father had assigned Him, Jesus dismissed His spirit into the Father's care. His body truly died and was committed to the grave, but His spirit was given over to the Father's keeping until the third day when once more it was reunited with His body—a body gloriously transformed and vested with power no human being had ever possessed. One reason this thrills our hearts is that we know our own resurrected bodies will be similar to His in many ways.

Now hear this: When Jesus said, *The Good Shepherd gives His life for the Sheep,* I believe He also meant *and I give them eternal life.* It is not just that our sins were taken away by His death, but life is imparted to us through His resurrection.

Those of us who are older and whose days on earth are nearing their appointed end, may by God's grace and in the name of our dear Savior also say, "Father, into Thy hands we commend our spirits." For us, it will be a matter of accepting God's good timing. For Jesus, it was by His own timing and by His own will, in perfect agreement with the Father's will and appointment, that He said these words.

The amazing results of these words of power and all they meant

1. *The testimony of the Roman centurion.* The Roman officer who led the execution squad heard and saw all that happened on the cross. He saw the way Jesus responded to the taunts of the accusing crowds. He heard every word Jesus spoke, both to man and God. He witnessed the somber darkness which spread over the land, and felt the earth quake. Even as Jesus yielded up His spirit to the Father, the centurion voiced his amazing verdict on all that had transpired: *Truly this was a righteous man who is the Son of God.*

2. *The rending of the temple veil.* Of all the incredible things that happened when Jesus died, the tearing of the veil in the temple was the most dramatic. We dare not miss the significance of this for our salvation and ongoing sanctification. There were two veils in the temple, but the one mentioned here separated the Holy Place from the Holy of Holies. That inner veil excluded worshipers from God's immediate presence. Only the high priest could go behind that veil, and then only once each year. Each of the three synoptic Gospels makes it clear that this rending of the veil occurred at the moment of Jesus' death. Thus through His death, the way into the heavenly sanctuary was opened.

The temple veil was heavy, and very strong. Only the hand of God could have torn it so completely and so easily, and only God's hand could open the way into His holy presence, which the tearing of the veil symbolized. The next time you read the book of Hebrews, especially chapter 4:16 and 9:19-20, you will have a much clearer understanding of what the Apostle meant by these words.

3.   *The end of the darkness.* The Gospel writers make it clear that the darkness lasted from noon until 3 p.m., but apparently the darkness was lifted as soon as Jesus died.

As soon as you understand that He died for you by command from God the Father, the sooner the darkness of doubt and fear will be driven from your heart. The power of His atoning death is the only thing that can break the power of darkness in your life, allowing the everlasting light of salvation to flood your soul and guide you safely home.

Yes, we believers may walk in darkness at times, overwhelmed by our fears and failures, and so deeply aware of our unworthiness. Don't promise God you will never sin again, for you will, but claim the power of Christ's words from the cross and humbly seek a closer, deeper walk with Him.

It is clear that each of the eleven true disciples received the blessed bread and wine from the hand of Jesus. It is also clear that all of them forsook Him and fled that very same night. But praise God that we know they all later returned, chastened, forgiven and restored. And so may you, even now, even here. The way is open because Jesus said. *Father, into thy hands I commend My spirit.*

www.ingramcontent.com/pod-product-compliance
Lightning Source LLC
Chambersburg PA
CBHW060622030426
42337CB00018B/3152